Little Pebble™

Healthy Me

I STAY ACTIVE

by Martha E. H. Rustad

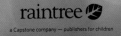

raintree
a Capstone company — publishers for children

Raintree is an imprint of Capstone Global Library Limited, a company incorporated in England and Wales having its registered office at 264 Banbury Road, Oxford, OX2 7DY – Registered company number: 6695582

www.raintree.co.uk
myorders@raintree.co.uk

Edited by Shelly Lyons
Designed by Juliette Peters
Picture research by Jo Miller
Production by Tori Abraham

ISBN 978 1 4747 3484 4
20 19 18 17 16
10 9 8 7 6 5 4 3 2 1

British Library Cataloguing in Publication Data
A full catalogue record for this book is available from the British Library.

Acknowledgements
Images by Capstone Studio: Karon Dubke
Photo Styling: Sarah Schuette and Marcy Morin

Printed and bound in China.

Contents

Move!

I want to stay healthy!

I move a lot each day.

My body stays active.

School

I go outside at playtime.

I hang from the monkey bars.

My muscles stay strong.

My class does P.E.

We play tag.

Running keeps
my heart healthy.

Practice

I go to football practice.

We play a game.

I save a goal!

My sister is a gymnast.

I cheer for her.

She does a flip!

My brother swims.

He goes to a swimming club.

He swims fast.

15

Outdoors

In winter we go sledging.

We climb up a steep hill.

I sledge down.

Whee!

In summer we go hiking.

We find a path and walk.

We stop to drink water.

I play at the park.

I keep my body moving.

Staying active means

a healthy me!

Glossary

active being busy and moving around

heart a muscle that moves blood in your body

hike to go for a long walk outside

muscle a band of body tissues that help the body move

playtime a break during school; students often go outside at playtime.

Find out more

Books

Exercising (Take Care of Yourself!), Sian Smith (Raintree, 2013)

Keeping Fit (Let's Read and Talk About), Honor Head (Franklin Watts, 2014)

Exercise (Being Healthy, Feeling Great), Robyn Hardyman (Wayland, 2012)

Websites

kidshealth.org/en/kids/stay-healthy/
Tips on keeping fit and having fun.

www.bbc.co.uk/guides/zxvkd2p
A video shows you how to stay healthy.

www.childrensuniversity.manchester.ac.uk/interactives/science/exercise/
Find out why exercise is so important.

Comprehension questions

1. On page 18, what do they stop to do?

2. Why is it important to keep your heart healthy?

3. What are muscles? Why are your muscles important?

Index